salmonpoetry

Publishing Irish & International
Poetry Since 1981

CU00921814

The
Gun
My
Sister
Killed
Herself
With

Daniel
Lawless

Published in 2018 by
Salmon Poetry
Cliffs of Moher, County Clare, Ireland
Website: www.salmonpoetry.com
Email: info@salmonpoetry.com

Copyright © Daniel Lawless, 2018

ISBN 978-1-910669-48-8

All rights reserved. No part of this publication may be reproduced or transmitted in any form or by any means, electronic or mechanical, including photography, recording, or any information storage or retrieval system, without permission in writing from the publisher. The book is sold subject to the condition that it shall not, by way of trade or otherwise, be lent, resold or otherwise circulated without the publisher's prior consent in any form of binding or cover other than that in which it is published and without a similar condition, including this condition, being imposed on the subsequent purchaser.

COVER AND INTERIOR DESIGN: *David Breskin*
TYPESETTING: *Siobhán Hutson*

Printed in Ireland by Sprint Print

To Johnny and Betty, Micky, Maureen, Terry—and Donna

Contents

Introduction   11

"A"   17

1.

Velda the Seer   21
Antoinette in Flames   22
Central State Hospital Visit, October 1962   23
In the Alzheimer's Ward of Saint Jude's   25
To the Motherland   26
Ant   27
October Fly   28
Exuscitatio   29
View from a Treehouse   30
Untitled, But Maybe   32
Shquiver (Dead Squirrel #1)   33
Phantom Limb   34
Portrait of My Father   35
To David   36
"Roll Caps"   38
"Schizophrenia"   39
Depression   41
Jenga   42
Cancer   43
Young Squirrel (Dead Squirrel #2)   44

2.

Kenjataimu	47
The Gun My Sister Killed Herself With	48
Dépaysement	49
What the Visitor Saw	50
My Conversation with FK	51
Books and Correspondences:	
A Short History of Decay, E.M. Cioran	52
Up Late	53
Flense	55
Paranoia	56
At a Dig in Kent	57
Gazebo	58
Dear Dewi	59
1982	61
Driving Lessons: How to Drive (A Prius)	62
Wig Shop Choir	64
The Memory of My Memory is My Memory	65
Unknown Destination	67
The Dean Has No Comment	68
Squat	69
The Shoes of the Old Ones	71
For a Forties Reading Lamp	72

3.

"buzz of the streetlamp—"   75

The Old Woman Hit by a Truck   76

Driving Lessons: How to Drive (Angry)   77

Sign Above a Discount Mattress Store,
    Strip Mall, Forktown, Alabama   79

Between Heaven and Hell   80

The Old Masters   83

Vine   85

Toro   86

Natural Selection   87

Books and Correspondences: Leviathan, *Thomas Hobbes*   88

Down in the Mangroves   90

Metope, Tagalog, Raskolnikov   92

Race Relations   93

Walk Out of Yourselves!   94

Segway   95

A Facebook Diorama   96

Querying the Hive Mind   97

4.

Transmission   101
A Poetry Reading on the Patio Outside the Tallahassee Room
    of the St. Petersburg Public Library   102
Endless Tuesday   104
Remedy   105
To Some Non-Letters, Praise   107
King of Pain   108
Poem with Horse and RB   109
The Poetry Assessor   111
Over Northern Virginia, October 18, 2016   113
Reading Rilke   117
A Clue, A Sign, A Bad Omen   118
Midpoint   119

Acknowledgments   120
About the author   123

Introduction

In *The Gun My Sister Killed Herself With* Danny Lawless writes unflinchingly as a self-witness, testifying in poem after poem that the unexamined life isn't only not worth living, but not worth reading about as well. Lawless excavates his past, from childhood on, from what Philip Larkin called "a unique distance from his own isolation." This "unique distance" Lawless writes from informs the sublime tone in many of his poems with a fearless focus on the idea that "home is so sad", which is, in fact, the title of a Larkin poem Lawless quotes in one of his epigraphs for the book. In language that often resonates as an admixture of James Joyce and Sylvia Plath, while managing to divine its own tragic/comic originality, Lawless leads his reader through loss, trauma, and illnesses with a truly remarkable expenditure of narrative and lyrical language, verbal music, and risible leaps, as in these heartbreaking lines from "Portrait of My Father":

> Cancer, April. Or May, The parlor swooned. By June
> His raw lips were a flea circus. Morphine
> And soon that jutting
> Lawless chin and half his jaw lopped off—a map
> Of olde Eire jammed on his shoulders
> I'd trace with curious fingers
> From Kinsale to Letterkenney
> As he dozed chair-bound halfway into *Benny Hill*. October
> In memory means standing straight as line-poles
> At his casket against the garlic gales
> Of Monseigneurs Castelli's Lord's prayer, our threadbare
> Sunday bests smelling of his forsaken Erinmore. The rest
> Half forgotten. Photographs interred in plastic jackets.
> Christmas, wistful. Snowflakes. School, our silent friends.
> Birthday Masses with old women in black dresses, Ma chirping,
> He's with the angels, et cetera, we were Irish.

This pitch-perfect vignette with aptly enjambed lines that betray the run-on, broken expression of the speaker descends the page with wrenching velocity. Indeed, even Lawless seems to have trouble keeping up with the pace of his memory's recall of immense particulars, which, in concert with his wit, lead him to such self-evident but resonant conclusions as that "we were Irish." But it's Lawless's "cold eye" that creates the necessary "unique distance from [his] own isolation," allowing him to regard himself as "another" with accurate empathy, as in these lines from his poem "'Schizophrenia'" which, earlier, speaks of his mother's reaction to the word that defined her son's life :

> She pushed open the heavy door—
> Watching her pause as she did, but tried to hide
> From us on unfamiliar busy street corners downtown,
> Waiting for the red light to turn and even then
> Looking both ways, ashamed and terrified.

Employing a strategy of lists and fugues, Lawless conjures details and images in his poems that capture heartrending scenes that conclude with cathectic power. In his poem 'Central State Hospital Visit, October 1962," for instance, he recalls a visit with his sister on her mental ward. But rather than merely describe her disease as a medical condition, he names the disease "terror," then relies on a series of images rather than medical language to convey both the psychic and visceral pain of *her* nascent schizophrenia.

> ...or was it "Terror"—whispered only to you?
> Your brow furrowing, your gaze
> Lifted beyond us hardened
> Into a squint
> As at a blank page, another hot-boxed Salem a crayon
> Firing *here* and *here* every malevolent stone,
> Fallen leaf or high star
> It found there,
> Flame Red Flame Red Flame Red its furious tip.

Throughout this ambitious book that's divided into four full sections, Lawless writes with *sprezzatura* and erudition about a vast spectrum of subjects and people, ranging from Rilke, Hobbes, Robert Bly, Facebook, and natural selection, to the old masters, a sign above a discount mattress store, a truck accident, sex abuse, Litost ("a state of paralyzing torment created by the sudden sight of one's own torment"), driving lessons, the flense, an imaginary conversation with Franz Kafka, *dépaysement*, cancer, jenga (the Swahili word for build), and the gun of the title poem, which "weighed as much / As an average newborn U.S. baby."

Lawless' disinterested, brazen eye emboldens him to break through propriety with a license afforded him less by the truths he tells than by how he tells them.

—Chard deNiord

Il ne faut pas s'astreindre à une oeuvre, il faut seulement dire quelque chose qui puisse se murmurer à l'oreille d'un ivrogne ou d'un mourant.

One must not confine oneself to an *oeuvre*, one must only say something that can be whispered in the ear of a drunkard or a dying man.

—E.M. Cioran

The essence of what I desire is simply this: to sleep away life.

—Fernando Pessoa, *The Book of Disquiet*

Home is so Sad
—Philip Larkin

Home is so sad. It stays as it was left,
Shaped to the comfort of the last to go
As if to win them back. Instead, bereft
Of anyone to please, it withers so,
Having no heart to put aside the theft

And turn again to what it started as,
A joyous shot at how things ought to be,
Long fallen wide. You can see how it was:
Look at the pictures and the cutlery.
The music in the piano stool. That vase.

"A"

Almost, the therapist would say,
Almost. Dear Angie, a paid optimist.
And so again she'd slide the pen
And paper across the sunroom table. The first
At first held up-side down for
A moment or simply dropped or flung
Aside. The second a thing mostly just stared at.
Again, the pen, the paper.
April, May, June, July—months of bitten, broken,
Aligned to probe an earhole with,
A crumpled morsel to be tasted or swallowed until
Aglow late one afternoon
Angie rushes out to greet us with what looks like
A toddler's tepee slashed once in rage incarnate—the letter
"A" as adduced by my father after his third stroke.
Also per Klaus, the King of Chimpanzees, in his cage
At the *International de Paris* in 1937—held up for the crowd—
Étonnant! Neither of which was ever followed by
Another letter, let history record, let alone a word.
Alone—yes. Side by side, as I've placed them. Their scanned
And printed-out facsimiles
Affixed with thumbtacks to the whitewashed wall
Above my desk, the silence there
A silence my shadow-head leans into, listening.
As if someday an answer will emerge from it:
        which the more pitiable.
Ah, no. The more les *dieux* absents. The more complete.

1

Velda the Seer

We all have a little fortuneteller in us,
She would say, years later, recalling
The day Mick, my sister's wounded punk/gear-head
Boyfriend in the seventies, *vamooshed*
For good again, hauling ass Killing Joke blaring
Down Eleanor in his Camaro straight-pipe;

Touching my own cheek as she says this, as if she can see
The red palm slap there, courtesy
Of Raymond, sweet sweater-y sexagenarian
Raymond. The red palm slap and the bruise
That bloomed beneath the bruise
And the one beneath that one.

Antoinette in Flames

Granted you were poor, great-grandmother,
And so accustomed to waiting.
Also that maybe the old backyard kiln
Had been hot enough once
To fire your little pots and bread
But not the right thing for bodies.
Who knew? Whose idea?
That idiot Eusebius? Half-crazy Donato?
Brunetta with her crew of drunk *camionisti?*
I heard it took three of them to break your legs
With a lug wrench to get you in there.
Four hours, five, six—
The speeches, the stories, the wine, the platters
Of *salsiccia con peperoni and sfogliatelle* disappeared
Or spilled to the dogs as drunk cousins
And their bored children took turns
Pulling faces at the little isinglass window.
Until even you had had enough—
According to Tancredo who
Saw it with his own eyes—
Rising slowly for a moment
With your back arched as if to sit up
In bed to scold them once more as you used to.
As you used to those last late summer afternoons,
Hearing Geraldo call at the door, back from
Mizda with a picnic basket and his head still on.
Sei pronta, mia colomba? Are you ready, my dove?
Sì, sì, solo un minuto …

Central State Hospital Visit, October 1962

You and I, big sister, giggling, in your room,
A Saturday, my eighth birthday.
On the crocheted bedspread
Between us a new box of 64 Crayolas
And a *Seek And Find* book opened
To "Musical Instruments"—
A Christmas scene for some reason
Full of hidden cellos and tubas,
Santa with a tiny saxophone
Entangled in his beard peeking up
Between two snare-drum barrels
At candy cane piccolos.
"A world to be unmasked," you murmur *sotto voce*—
A term of course
I don't know yet, scribbled Mountain Meadow
Scarlet, Burnt Sienna, Denim.

In two months, though I can't know this
Yet either, you'll be a perpetual motion
Smoking machine dressed in a body, glazed and amped
To the hair ends thanks to Haldol, thin in a thin
Bathrobe with an adhesive taped
Pocket labeled "Maureen."

Dusk falling, and *your* birthday now,
As in "Birthday"—curls of green
Ribbon, boxes with new sweaters and mittens,
A coconut cake with jimmies and sixteen candles.
Each item discovered and colored in
With a glance but missing the theme.

… Or was it "Terror"—whispered only to you?
Your brow furrowing, your gaze
Lifted beyond us hardened
Into a squint
As at a blank page, another hot-boxed Salem a crayon
Firing *here* and *here* every malevolent stone,
Fallen leaf or high star
It found there,
Flame Red Flame Red Flame Red its furious tip.

In The Alzheimer's Ward at Saint Jude's

Stalling, not wanting to stare, I stare
Into the stately day-room's aquarium,
Une salle fantastique sous la mer
Un-updated since pin boys crouched on planks:
Drifts of plastic coral like multicolored mud, fake rocks,
A tiny wreck and treasure chest, the yellow ape
In cast iron boots I take to be my alternate
In uselessness. Wisps of something white
Have made a Q-Tip of his brandished spear.
I've brought lemon drops, kind words,
A picture book of polar bears.

Long seconds pass.

Tap, Tap. Smudge a finger round the glass
To rouse the occupants.
Nothing. A vacant glance, and gone. The same, or nearly,
As if I'd turned instead behind me and
Rapped upon a wide forehead—
All those bright echoing rooms
Where nameless children play or ghostly tulips bloom,
A green squawking stalks its perch
Above a grand odd-shaped thing.

To The Motherland

I was so strong, our grandfather would say,
Flexing his sagging bicep like a spinach-less Popeye

Full of *Tovarich* as he pushed back from the table
And lit up an unfiltered Camel.

I had the will of a knife, he'd say sometimes, too,
Waxing poetic as he repeated it

In the oddly formal diction he employed
After a few hours spent philosophizing

In the Vodka House with the other old Russian
Generals, ex-spies or bagmen, to hear him tell it,

Who back in the day did terrible things to innocent people
For the Party (I'm summarizing)

And regretted them
If regretting is a shoulder shrug

Over a half-eaten cheese pirozhki. (I'm imagining.)
Once—and only once—I stopped by there after school

To pet Fyodor, a twenty-year-old cat
According to my grandfather.

His paws and shameless face were smeared with blood.
There was something shadowy under the table.

The terrible scraping sound of chairs,
And then the other part of the proclamation,

Soaring over my head: I had the will of a knife
In the hands of a child. (I'm dreaming.)

Ant

I confess it was I
Who stole a bag of hosts
From the sacristy
And ate them for breakfast
With a bottle of chocolate milk
Behind the dentist's office.

Who in eighth grade got a blowjob
From Angela
In the choir loft
One stormy spring afternoon
While the faces
Of your fiery prophets
Darkened with rage.

I, who stole twenty tabs of hydrocodone
From Gramma
When she had all her teeth pulled.
Not to mention her car,
Which I wrecked and left somewhere in Tampa.

I who so many things.

Yet still you find me,
Lord,
This fine October morning
Head bowed
Before the sports pages.

You who are the author
Of my most intimate desires
Ringing your bell
As if I were a child at recess,
And sending I see your most esteemed
Black-robed emissary
To fetch me.

October Fly

The terror of the spider's web
Was somebody else's, apparently.

Likewise that flat, low-hanging cloud
That followed your dear cousin
Halfway down the bar.

And the little one, what's his name?
He hasn't come home from school,
And now it's getting dark,

His mother's busy explaining
To the jittery sheriff who doesn't appear
To be listening—

When suddenly he, too,
Has somewhere else to be!

Exuscitatio

—to my mother in the Memory Care Unit at Saint Mary's

So serious, gentle seeming, thoughtless smile
And pearled brow, the held breath of her gaze,
Glazed ringlets framing newly
Roseate cheeks, pale hands
Like doves flown to rest on her lap
Through the half-opened window—
How is it, one thinks, this child is dead?
That a post behind her splayed feet rises
Beneath her scissored frock with metal clamps
Scirssored at the waist and neck, while stiff wires
Snake her sleeves to hold bloodless arms
In place? The pupils of her wide eyes painted
On closed eyelids? How possible,
The mind asks, the impossible minutes passed
In that impossible room—the photography studio
Of one R. Dechavannes, sweet and parlous
With eau de toilette, its bald and everywhere-scrim
Of unnamable dirt,
This Paris morning in July, 1887?
How could love—love!—demand even *this*?
To which the heart answers,
Exuscitatio—with its own nagging question:
Didn't you write
That epigraph, Daniel?

View from a Treehouse

Honestly, I don't remember that much about it.
The day you left home
With a busted lip and broken glasses
After standing up in high school
Math class screaming Masturbation
Is a sin! at some kid and being cold-cocked
I was like, *whatever*.
Although I didn't say, like whatever.
This was in the sixties. I was ten.
I had my friends, my new ice skates,
Whatever it was ten-year-olds had.
Maybe a treehouse.
Yes, definitely a treehouse—2x4s dragged
From the new subdivision going up
A few blocks over, scavenged half-used rolls of tar paper,
Squares of carpet inside from the pallets stacked up
Behind Len's—right,

I can see it all again
Now, the sycamore tree trunk rising straight up
Through the roof, rope ladder, everything rusted,
Damp, the Emerson transistor radio
Tuned to WAKY to hear Weird Beard spin
"Love Me Do" every hour.
Bobby and I fumbling limp Marlboros in mittens
While we watched through the spy-slot
We'd sawed with a steak knife into a gap
Between two sheets of plywood spiked with nails
As Mom and Dad guided you like a blind man
Into the back seat of the green Dodge.
Your fifteen-year-old face freckled
In the window with sleet, fat and pale, wearing
That everything-inside-crouched-and-wary look
Tim Tam got at the vet, maybe trembling, whatever
The onset of schizophrenia looks like

To a ten-year-old who views it from a tree house
Through a spy-slot sawed with a steak knife into a gap
Between two sheets of plywood spiked with nails.

And can I say again that I—that boy—
Really didn't care much
One way or the other if his only brother
Never came back again,
Barely gave a second thought to his swollen lip
Let alone tried to imagine for one minute
The soul-rasping taunts and torments
That must've been skirling behind his taped-up glasses
As he was hustled off into oblivion,
That he had his friends and ice skates,
His treehouse, his cigarettes and Beatles,
Is this allowed? I ask you, not rhetorically or with anger
In my heart, Great Whoever or
However you are, but merely as a matter
Of curiosity, after fifty years doesn't the statute
Of limitations apply here? Isn't this just the way
Of things? Yes or no? And if the latter, whatever
Made you think you could get away with such horseshit?

Untitled, But Maybe

Reveriries ar fugit sectare
If you want to go full Catholic, circa 1961.
How we adored me
As you lay your soft hands so softly

        there and *there*,

Traipsing a fine path
From pink cheekbone to sparse jet
Pubis with shaky fingers;
Pleasure sin trebled
As we stood before your rectory
Bedroom mirror. O Father—O Jerry—
Musty and mustachioed, six Stroh's
To the wind, how your shame
Inflamed me, became me,
Became mine.

Shquiver (Dead Squirrel #1)

A word I made up for the thing I did
After I did what I did to the squirrel

Half in light half in darkness
In the ditch with its dry rivulets of gravel

Where I crouched and looking up
Read the puffed letters of my own name

Ensnared in spiked graffiti
On the Reverend Sherman J. Minton Bridge.

Phantom Limb

Every day the same clipped-on bow tie,
Same unpronounceable name.
Mrs. Kearns told us the whole story,
But we preferred our own.
A machete, an alligator.
Okay, Okay.
Behind the incinerator, we made you
Let us feel the stump.
Make it wiggle, we'd say,
Shake my hand.
Okay.
That was pretty funny.
But we had other things to do,
Like pulling down the retard's pants.
You ate sardines for lunch,
Sat in the back row studying.

And that was that,
Except for a brief reprise when
The Beast with Five Fingers
Came out.
Is it going to strangle us? we gasped.
Can it play the piano?
What's it doing now?
It's giving you the finger.
It's scratching my balls.
Voice like a burned-out match.
Did I shiver? I shivered. And bought
K's *Basic Polish.*
In my room the next night
Pinned up my sweater sleeve,
Wrote *Kazimierz, Kochaam cie*—
I love you—
Fifty times left-handed in my notebook.

Portrait of My Father

Face forever dull scarlet, puckered when he snuffled
Up the last packed flakes of Erinmore
From one of his half-bents and gave it out as acrid
Comment on our clothes, my comics, Saint Michael's
Shoddy footwork on the pitch.
There was a pineapple on the tobacco tin.
According to him Virginia
Was full of them, and drunk Indians.
At eight, I kept ship's nails, odd stamps,
Two perfect ambered bees in one.
By twelve pinched coins against the day
I could train away from that ancient nobody. Then
Cancer. April. Or May. The parlor swooned. By June
His raw lips were a flea circus. Morphine,
And soon that jutting
Lawless chin and half his jaw lopped off—a map
Of olde Eire jammed on his shoulders
I'd trace with curious fingers
From Kinsale to Letterkenney
As he dozed chairbound halfway into *Benny Hill*. October
In memory means standing straight as line-poles
At his casket against the garlic gales
Of Monseigneur Castelli's Lord's Prayer, our threadbare
Sunday bests smelling of his forsaken Erinmore. The rest
Half forgotten. Photographs interred in plastic jackets.
Christmas, wistful. Snowflakes. School, our silent friends.
Birthday masses with old women in black dresses, Ma chirping
He's with the angels, et cetera, we were Irish.

To David

Sideswiped by Jamie, the forty-year-old drunk
Merry Mobile driver after school
And staggering over to our house half blind
His face smeared with cherry popsicle and sprinkled
With fine gravel though no charges were ever filed.
And to crazy old ex-Lieutenant Mr. Gallfly
In his garage lawnmower workshop
Who clocked Jimi square in the mouth with a lug wrench
For among other things being half-Jap.
To Tommy B's mother who peeled the skin
Off both his hands with hot coffee for swiping
Two boxes of Red Hots from Taylor's,
Not forgetting his lazy-eyed big sister Angela,
Who the next month leaped
From their third-story window
Breaking both ankles, cracking her sternum
And skull, who fifty years later likes the day nurse
To read her *Harry Potter* every afternoon after lunch.
To my twelve-year-old cousin Tommy L
Whose neighbor's dad showed him
How to jack off one afternoon in the basement,
As to the guy she told the cops smelled like Pine-Sol
And wore a blue tie and cufflinks
Who pulled Theresa R down an alley under the El
And stuck his cock in her mouth.
To Coach Albertus at Big Bend River
Showing off for some sorority girls
As he gunned the skiff's motor
That snatched one arm up to the elbow from Larry.
To all three of the brothers N who got to albino Billy
So bad he slit both wrists with the leg
Of a porcelain statue of Saint Joseph
After smashing it to bits on the floor,
And came to school the next day and showed us the cuts
He'd closed up with Superglue.

And last but not least to Alberto,
My best friend, who suffered
Like so many no visible injury but whose whole life
He once told me he knew was fucked
The minute his father climbed up on the roof
Of the windmill at Putt-Putt
Dangling the last Schlitz in a six-pack from his arm—
Who had just enough English
To inform our eighth-grade graduation party his wife was
A whore and we all could all kiss his ass,
And while he was at it did we know
Our precious little Alberta was a fag?
To the way when he'd finished he just stood there
Looking up to the sky with his arms spread out
As people do when they wonder *Why*,
Why about something and you know it,
That gesture, even if you're passing by in a car
Or too far away to hear them,
Know it as well as you know your own name
As they already know the answer.

Roll Caps

Five for a dollar. Rolled red paper strips in a red plastic box.
Each centered blister a potential bang.

Meant for cap guns—but whoever kept a cap gun
Around for long?

So you'd just roll them out on the sidewalk
And take a sharp rock to those suckers.

Pop! Pop! Pop!—you can still hear it.
Still see your bloody finger

As you hustled toward the garage
Your father already reaching over a *Playboy*

Past the morning's Schlitz cans for the handkerchief
Stiff with dried snot, poking out his shorts: *opere citato*

"Eleanor Avenue, Autumn, 1963," Plate 257,
In The Big Book of Obscure Childhood Sorrows.

"Schizophrenia"

Not the thing, but the word.
Often misused, like *surreal* when people in spotlights,
Barefoot, shake their heads

As they look back at their house
In flames, or breathless among friends recall
Exchanging a few words

With Jack White at a bar; in our house
After my brother's diagnosis, it became Mama's *cruccio*—
Her pet peeve. As a noun

It was a rectangular hole in the dictionary,
The jagged edges of pages 151-153
In The Wonderland of Knowledge.

But, oh, in its adjectival or adverbial form—
That's when the fireworks started. 34 across
In a crossword to improve her English—

"Like a two-headed monster"—
Meant a furious, scratching Bic, or *Congress
Is a bit schizophrenic on this issue …*

How her whole crumpled face
Would tighten up
Like a fist aimed at poor Roger Mudd.

Which was nothing compared to the bitter ire
Reserved later for the inevitable "schizophrenic"
Preceding *homeless man* or *serial murderer*—

A rage so inwardly extravagant, so invisibly
Arms flung out, head-clasping
Italianate overtaking her, her whole body

Trembled with it, afire as she pitched
The Courier, The Reader's Digest
Out our third-story window into the street.

"Schizofrenia" with its truffled *fr*, I heard *her* say,
Once and only once,
To the priest as I waited outside while the long line

Of our nosy neighbors grew longer
At the confessional on Good Friday; eight years old,
Fidgeting, the pew knotting my thighs,

My shoulders, until finally
She pushed open the heavy door—
Watching her pause as she did, but tried to hide

From us, on unfamiliar busy street corners downtown,
Waiting for the red light to turn and even then
Looking both ways, ashamed and terrified.

Depression

It's a bell curve, she's saying,
This sweet doctor
With chipped scarlet fingernails
And big hair
Mouthing and pointing
As she swoops a made-up deaf sign
For "hill"—some days she'll be

> *Here*, some *here*.

1960. In seven years
You'll be dead, my sister
The sister who killed herself at sixteen.
Paroxetine, ECT, Paroxetine,
Notebook paper pictures
Of bare trees and fanged lizards
In beige therapists' rooms
Our mute father
Will drive you to and from
In the pickup lie ahead.

But for now there's only
The three of us, M—
Staring at this phantom
Hill you're somewhere on—

> *There* or *there*—

A hill that isn't a hill at all but maybe a bell
In the other sense too—
Calling all the kids back
From recess, ringing in the schoolyard,
A bell you can't answer,
Just can't.

Jenga

Not a nonsense word—in Swahili it means *build*—
But as Chomsky writes, "highly associative."
Jenga, a painting by Basquiat.
I'm feeling a little *jenga* about myself today
Mutters Willy Loman.
That beater was *jenga*, bro!
Slang for certain amphetamines.
A '50s film set in a jungle
Starring an unsteady Ellen Drew
And 300 black-faced zombies.
The box caution-yellow with orange ray gun rays
Radiating from the center, a scarlet stripe at the bottom
Commanding, See How You Stack Up!
In jittery letters as if we needed it,
As if we weren't already always measuring,
Teetering, holding our breaths, *jenga*
In our trembling twelve-year-old hearts.

Cancer

The doctor finally says,
And suddenly
I'm bolting from the back seat

Of our fat red car
Towards a greener circle
In the green grass,

My father's voice somewhere
Off in the distance behind me.
What can I say?

I was three. I thought
The lily pads would hold me up
All the way to the other side.

Young Squirrel (Dead Squirrel #2)

The day after the day Dad left I found you
In the alley behind the Quik Stop
Way out by Aunt Rosarita's house,
Your black little back feet still peddling
Your invisible bicycle, your sharp teeth still gnawing
An invisible peanut. You gave up the ghost
Of sour cranberry juice to my nostrils. The nurse
In me was a book I never read so I thumbed
Your furred neck flecked with blood and flicked
The gnats from your eyeballs as best I could.

O, fallen squirrel angel
From squirrel heaven, scion of the great
Acrobat family *Sciurius*—for a moment, after,
I considered a squirrel funeral like the one my sister staged
For our old tabby Tim Tam—bunched Kleenex
In a hatbox, Our Fathers, a solemn march
With scarlet tapers to the foot of a flowering coffee tree.
But you were just a squirrel, and I was ten,
Helpless, far from home and furious inside
And the dumpster was so close.

2

Kenjataimu

The apple is split.
But still the thrown knife quivers.

The Gun My Sister Killed Herself With

Was a cubit long and weighed half as much
As an average newborn U.S. baby.
Who sold it to her remains a matter of police conjecture,
A "collector," most likely, or a friend in need
Of cash—no receipt ever surfaced.
What she did between the time she got it and the act
Adds little to the picture: coffee at McDonalds,
A few words exchanged with a balding man in an Army
Jacket outside the 7-Eleven on Broadway, no phone calls,
No letter. When my mother got the news
She was hanging sheets to dry on the backyard
Clothesline—neighbors heard her
Cry two blocks over and thought a cat had died.
(Where, exactly, Father spent that afternoon: c.f.
Conjecture.) How Irish-pretty she was, pale, petite,
Kind, smart and slyly funny are duly noted now on
Her birthday, in photographs and little tales
That end in tears that end in silence: we the cage
And Rilke's panther pacing there, a thousand bars
And beyond the bars no world but why.

Dépaysement

French: The feeling of being in a foreign place, exile

—for Thierry R

For three days you were like a piece of ripe fruit
Falling through a tree of many sharp branches.

But what could I do? Ice chips, damp washcloths …
Finally, the halls grew quiet,

The doctors, even the nurses departed.
It was just the two of us. Ouagadougou

Muted on CNN World cantilevered above the visitor's chair:
A woman on a ragged pallet kept touching her face

As if she were afraid she'd left it
At the night market that kept exploding

And recomposing itself. Her eyes were closed,
Her piebald head moved ever so slightly—

A French tourist reached out to console her.
Out of the corner of my eye

While I was stroking your vanishing hair
I saw his disembodied hand

Among many others so thin and black
They might have been sticks.

I'm sorry, he kept mouthing
When the camera drew back—*Je suis désolé*—

The way his lips moved—
A little like your word *dépaysement*.

We didn't speak the language.

What the Visitor Saw

Fräulein Pfaff—fifteen, sixteen?
Radiant, psychotic.
Shivering, shirtless,
Baring her teeth
To tear at the flesh of a potato
Pulled from the side garden
As the black clouds burst:

Her breasts and pink nipples
As she heaved
Back her shoulders
To spit out the filthy peel
Pale like the stern preacher's kids
Mocking him in the village
With their tongues stuck out—
The kind one wants to twist
By the ear
When no one is looking.

My Conversation with FK

"You do not need to leave your room …
the world will freely offer itself to you …
It has no choice."

Maybe, Franz, but right now I'm dying
For a Blueberry Big Gulp and a pack of Camels.
And after that there's the dry cleaning and the vet,
Aunt Betty who wants her email back, garlic hummus
At Trader's Joe's for my vegan son, you get the picture.
I really *do* have to leave my room, although I'm pretty sure
That's not your point.
On the other hand, I too am literally dying:
Cancer, esophageal.
Dark days. Like you in your last months I cannot eat.
Still, out I go. The cost of doing business.
How you kept on writing, letter after letter,
Making small talk with Brod and Dora
As you inched your way around
The park across from *der Sterbehaus*—
It's not beyond me, now, you know.
But, oh—these grey skies, K—so cold.
The autumn leaves, their emptiness, their pity.

Books and Correspondences: *A Short History of Decay*, E.M. Cioran

A flock of *Aratinga nenday* in the park today—
Green parakeets, so exactly the color of the grass
The grass itself seemed to screech.
And all at once fly away.
A wonderful thing to imagine:
A magic carpet, no Ali Baba.
Just the shriekshape of it
Swooping and curling, rising free of the earth.
Then no carpet—
Disappeared over the treetops, the water tower
Where an intoxicated boy, your neighbor's son,
Once clawed the glistening sides shrieking
In the dead of night until he drowned.
As if—still—you needed reminding:
By all evidence we are in this world to do nothing.

Up Late

This morning, leather-gloved against blisters
And armed with my aunt's grand new Flexrake Basket
LRB 140—an impromptu visit to their old housekeeper
Florene's rusting doublewide
To pick lychee nuts, which I've never tasted
But my uncle Bob assures me I will love
Shaved into coconut pudding and topped with something
He calls his Lychee Love Sauce.
She's not home, of course, Florene: colon cancer.
Two years ago now. A long haul, her black-haired widower
Concedes, polite but staring straight ahead
Over the dashboard, waving us on as he backs the pickup
Down the cracked asphalt drive.

It's hard. Harder than I would have thought.
Twenty minutes maybe half an hour of swatting punkies
Twisting our doughy necks and arms into soft pretzels,
Working the spring-loaded jaws so they claw
The stems without breaking the rind and then suddenly rain
That pulls us toward the carport: smokes, Cokes in a cooler
Where we'd left them,
Tired chitchat between rolls of thunder as we lament
The sorry state of Florene's garden, until turning back
We spot a dazed figure on the neighbor's lawn.

Sylvie, Clara summarizes—grandniece, 16,
Drugs—as we watch her watch us, unseeing, cheeks smeared
With mud, slow-dancing to *la musique inouïe*,
Fiddling with a garter snake, making a bracelet, a necklace.
She's beautiful, wearing nothing but a man's swimming trunks.

And shall I speak now, Reader, of the rain that never ended?
Our rolled-shoulder dash through it
To the car as we left her to her reveries, Florene's doublewide
Receding through the fogged-over rear window
As we bumped back down the gravel road,
The tart, almost candy scent of what lychees we'd gathered
Squirming out through the twig holes punched
In the single Winn Dixie bag we'd managed to fill?
The darkness of the kitchen as we spilled them on the counter
Where Bob stood with his Oxy peeler,
The slow brush of his forearm as he swept
The rough pinkred of their hides into the sink
To expose balls of translucent flesh,
How we waited as he ground them with fresh coconut flakes
And poured a steady stream of heavy cream and egg yolks
Into a bowl, then spooned that warm pudding up with plastic forks
From Hardees, the rain finally diminishing
To plump drops plopping from the gutter?

Or are you still thinking about that half-dressed dancing girl
With her scorched toddler mind, how childishly elegant she was
Making jewelry out of a snake? The aroma of her pale breasts
And the illicit pleasure of kissing them,
Taking them topped with Lychee Love Sauce into your mouth?

Flense

To flinch, to tense?
A scam, back in the day.
Or a surgical procedure:
Stripping the oleaginous
Stratum basale.
Unrelated to the French
Word for arrow, *flèche.*
A grove, or a copse.
Opulent, dense.

Paranoia

Who says the owl
In my head.
All night,
Twisting his neck...

I can feel it.
His mounting fright—
Who goes there?
Who?

In the daytime too.

At a Dig in Kent

No ring or amulet adorns their lovers' sleep,
No shield or sword protects it
From some forgotten foe.
Just this tarp that lets the daybright drizzle in
And a modest clasp that shines
Like a coin dropped into a fountain
Where *gli amaniti* light as angels peer
Into their future bathed in tears
Of sunlit spray.

How he whispers
In her ear sweet truly nothings now,
The ardent hand that cups her vacant breast
Still full of fresh passion,
The girlish twist of her ancient hips.
So barely there
Their dreams outweigh them.

Gazebo, Town Square

From here, it appears
As a cage someone has left
Momentarily on a baize tabletop,

Domed, and set with a swing
Where our silver-crested local lovebirds' coo and peck
Has lately been reduced to one

Who coos and pecks no more, but carries on
In pantomime the essential conversation—
Or yawps in scarlet startled grief

That unspools into a kind of wary meditation
On bright details I know but barely see
From the courthouse steps:

Sea-green brooch, a waggled key,
The tooth-split, sun-seized carapace of sunflower seed
Chirped upon cloud-stained stone.

Dear Dewi

—Koh Pu, Thailand, 53 Kilometers from Phuket, 2015

At the end of this sentence I will remember you,
I promise, but after eleven long years
Let me linger here on the terrace
For a few moments longer
Digesting Poom's mind-blowing *Khao khluk kapi*
With three fingers of good bourbon as Camille
The hotel cat sways beside me
In the hammock to the last *surr-ays*
Of "Stone Soul Picnic" floating up
Like the aroma of lemon lip gloss
From the poured plastic rock speakers,
While above my chest one by one StarChart
Summons spectral bears and shepherds
From the night sky with a slow sweep of my iPhone;
Let the breeze that ruffles my shirt and trousers
When I remove them to swim sail my skin
Softly as the shadows of lace curtains,
Or when I decide against it and lie back down,
As recompense for growing old and fat
Permit me instead to indulge in the brief delight
Of shivering not from cold but from conjuring
From the restless clatter of palm fronds
Up the beach a strange city out of Calvino
Where "constant duels" are fought by ghosts
With rusty swords on nameless squares;
Then when my memories come, as they must,
Let them be faded, and bowdlerized,
Or redacted as in some ancient CIA document,
Resembling nothing more sinister than the slow
Passage of exotic stamps from countries long passed
Into oblivion beneath a bronze lamp
In an old moldy study;

And when the liquor kicks in let my dreams
Be of soft caresses and paternal kisses
That flare up and flower behind my eyes
Like phosphorescent pomegranates,
Before I wake pleasantly hazed, a kid
Before The Great Cosmo's magic wand,
Unsure if he has suddenly appeared,
Or disappeared; in other words

Let me not be the kind of man
Who drifts from room to room
Like a fine localized drizzle, as I often do now,
Or wears time like a dark suit
Inside his body, but rather, as what? trade in kind
For these ten years plus one I've survived
On this goddamned planet,
Perhaps a freshly minted superhero
Or the astonished inheritor
Of ten thousand billion dollars, whatever
Would be enough to let me fly backwards in time
And protect those I loved from everything
I couldn't protect them from then—
The crystalline allure
Of suddenly exposed seafloor,
Mute klaxons and absent seismometers,
Liars in shirt-jacs dining on foie gras
Heaped on toast points behind
Iron fences strung with barbed wire;
The godless wind, the wave,
Dear Dewi, that staggered up the dock,
The flimsy shanty's steps,
A drunk to knock his wife around, a turquoise bear
Your new son had never seen,
That licked his honeyed smile and ate him.

1982

The year many found the needle but lost the thread.
When what was lost, stayed lost. AIDS. Rhodesia.
Start of the Weather Channel. Man
Of the Year—The Computer. The year after the year
Ronald Reagan swept
49 states and John Lennon died.
Quik Stops by then everywhere selling *Imagine*
Etched on grey stones at the counter.

Driving Lessons: How to Drive (A Prius)

—for Coralette

Own it. You're white, Gen X, rich
In most of the world—so forget
The COEXIST sticker,
The hip tip to Black Lives Matter,
And focus on the asset at hand:
Not the MPG or the environment—
That battery will end up in a landfill—
But silence. That kid
On the skateboard you scared halfway back
To the South Side when you rolled up
Like a ghost on split rims
Through his earbuds on Halsted?
The look on his face
As if he'd traced a cartoon *Home Alone* face
On cardboard and stuck it square
On his shoulders: *Booyah!* You can't buy
That kind of shit. Or maybe you can. Just you
In the cockpit of a slow stealth jet on four wheels,
An upgrade from the low roar
Of that cracked engine Escort
To a magic carpet with seats lined with faux leather
To carry you as they say in Alabama
Where you're from to the well and back
And then some. Tuscaloosa in the rearview
On the test drive as you stopped
On the side of a road, out where the traffic
Thinned past the John Deere and the Walgreens
And just sat there, listening to the faint tocks
Of June bugs on the windshield—a replay
Of that last day, your drunk stepdad
Hollering down three flights to the kitchen
To get up there, his voice tailing off
To some weird Morse code pocked out in your ear

You decoded fast as threat, as in touch,
As in run, so you did. All the way to Chicago
Where he's that homeless guy now, making tracks in thin air
As you unpack his backpack right there on the curb,
Or that punk mapped in tats in Grant Park
Splashed like cold-brew on the hood
Before he gets up and squeaks *Fuck Yous!*
Spinning off in the heat. The day tall
As the Sears Tower rising up all around you,
Coralette; you, getting it all back, and then some,
Eris in an apple-red Prius macking chaos
One by one on that lurid that absentee god.

Wig Shop Choir

You, for whom the bluebirds of happiness
Dress up as prison guards, turning and

Raising your arms—just now—in triumph,
Grasping a chicken leg gnawed to the bone.

Maestro
Of the wig shop choir!

I could almost hear it, the last glorious *F*
Hovering in the chilly night air

As I stepped into the crosswalk,
The mad king applauding

With his two red hands.

The Memory of My Memory is My Memory

We ran our trap lines according to Hoyle,
And forgot about them.
Set the goldfish on the table.
Back and forth you watched them swim
With that determined, frightened look they have,
Before we forgot about them, too.
We were dancing *Jarabe*, we were dancing The Shag.
The prairie was our ballroom.
Then a parking lot in Cupertino
Outside some kind of all-night dentist.
The next thing I knew we were up in the hills,
Staring at a doublewide with a busted door
And a mailbox that looked like it would choke
On a piece of good news.
From the shadow of a shriveled up orange tree
I watched you watch me watch you
Swaying ever so slightly on the left-behind swing set
As if one of us was already a ghost.
Which would have been fine, except we weren't yet.
We still had voices to yell with, and hands to shove with,
And fingers to make a sign
To sell the furniture and then the car with.
Our ears were in pretty good shape, too.
Even with towels stuffed under the bathroom door
Crack and pillows over our heads
We could hear footsteps on the gravel driveway
In the middle of the night
And somebody messing with the windows.
Not to mention our terrible smiles—
That time you prepared your famous *salade niçoise*
With eggs from the neighbor's coop
And lettuce and carrots with dirt still on them,
The bicycles that appeared out of nowhere!
How long it all seemed.

So that it wasn't exactly a disappointment
When one of us actually disappeared.
I remember the knife, the 12-inch TV sailing across
The porch like a rat with a long thin tail
Followed by the black cat you'd taken in.
And the racket—as if you were hammering a good-bye letter
With your fists against the walls.
At dawn, when I crept out to look,
Your footprints in the dew-soaked grass
Made a line like an exclamation mark
With a ball of wadded-up panties for the period.

Unknown Destination

Like one of the dead in Hans Memling's
Fifteenth-century vision
Of the Last Judgment, stepping from their graves as if
Onto a crowded stage,
Trailing their winding sheets like matted boas—

So you came to me in memory
As I leaned against a pole at the Bruges station,
Done in by the day's chilly museum crawl:

A farm boy Caesar staggered out for a piss
At a long ago fraternity party, missing your step
And tumbling into the pit
Your Brothers had dug for the next day's pig roast,
Cracking your skull on a knob of Kentucky limestone.

How you slumbered there and finally rose
Shakily among us in an unraveling toga,
Head cocked as if to the unheard music of a cloud
Of shivering trumpet vines,
Saint and devil by turns of the late-arriving, oldfangled
Ambulance's revolving eye.

The Dean Has No Comment

Seven, maybe eight years old, nude, and out
Of nowhere there she was
Streaked from the waist down in glistening
Pebbled green shit, shivering
As she ate a tube of cherry lip gloss
In the Great Ape House at the Lincoln Park Zoo.
My wife was the first to see her—
Her hand flying to her mouth.
A man in overalls, a boy
In a Nike tracksuit, two women
Wearing Amish bonnets,
Then the floodgates—a pack of Boy Scouts
Trailing what looked like plastic swords,
Half a dozen Hasidic Jews—no one touched her.
She might've been surrounded
By some kind of force field.
We all just stood there, each new arrival
Stunned, speechless,
So many hands flying up to so many mouths,
You'd think there'd be a word for it, the emotion,
For example, *Litost*,
Which Kundera describes as a "state of paralyzing torment
Created by the sudden sight of one's own misery,"
Something like that.
Even Otto, the Dean of Lowland Gorillas, 24
And having been a resident there since birth
According to the brochure,
Stopped scratching himself and looked out, through the bars,
With those brooding brown-black eyes gorillas have.
His hand, too, starting to rise upwards as if
—But then—a mighty yawn.

Squat

To chase the first-night jitters I drank apple wine
And stacked my fingers one atop the other
Like lobster claws and waved
Them over my head menacingly.
I stomped my feet
And made the rat turds dance.

An icy draft circled the room
Like a terrified bird.
The cupboards were bare, of course,
And so were the walls,
Except for the dime store Jesus
On the Cross somebody gave a hotfoot to.

        For a little while

I watched myself in a dark windowpane,
Turning pages struck golden by candlelight.
I could have been the Duc de Berry
Admiring a sun-kissed plow, a forest
Of turrets against an azure sky,
But I wasn't. Instead there was a photograph
Of a schoolboy raising a Kalashnikov over his head
While puffing on a huge cigar,

And later another one of a woman leaning forward
On a three-legged chair,
Holding beside her cheek like a puppet
A picture of her long-faced husband,
Their two mouths half open
To a street filled with burning garbage,
As if they'd both lurched up
Out of the same nightmare;

Moving before Him
In the wavering light,
First this way and then that,
Even The Lord Almighty
Looking a little nervous too, I noticed,
As if missing the company of the Good Thief,
And, then, even the Bad.

The Shoes of the Old Ones

Their makers vanished, along with the horses and clouds
That admired themselves in the cobbler's window.

The uppers of heavy tooled leather,
        like an old-fashioned valise or portfolio
Into which important papers are slipped,

Bruised with the seal of a bank, or even an empire.
Thick-soled, cut broad across the instep,

Bearing, if somehow held close, the expected scents
Of their human owners: sweetish and fearsome.

I see them lined up beneath the pews at church,
Like sentences in an archaic tongue,
        punctuated by the tips of canes.

For a Forties Reading Lamp

—from Material Elegies

Far from the fusty study with its sturdy desk
Where once you lent your Midas touch
To rotary phones and checkbooks,
Saudade hipsters in cardigans and twee fedoras now
Adore your swan-necked silhouette in Village vintage shops.
Amex, Uber, home and fit with an organic LED bulb,
The lucky couple leans you in just-so
Before a tintype of two staid bare-bodied *matelots*
Entwined on a Belle Époque daybed:
                    switched on
For the first time is it any wonder
Suddenly exposed in that cold new light
They seem as shocked as you are?

3

buzz of the streetlamp—
something greater than us
wants to come in

The Old Woman Hit by a Truck

—after Tranströmer

The old woman hit by a truck is just lying there,
On the sidewalk on Sixth Avenue.
Broken glasses, blood-flecked checked skirt hiked up,
Head turned impossibly sideways—Tranströmer
Got it right in "Vermeer" when he wrote, *It's not*
A sheltered world. In the picture a man's pant leg zooms
Over her pocketbook, three children's shadows hurry along
A wall. Although apparently these last seconds have not got
Permission to last for centuries—by the next day
Someone has Photoshopped an iPhone under her ear,
Captioned his masterpiece "Out of Service."
Thrown up on the web, everything in that image says,
I am not open, I am empty.

Driving Lessons: How to Drive (Angry)

Assuming you've sprung the keys from your purse
Or twigged where you tossed them like a fistful
Of silver cilantro in the *cazuela* on the credenza,
And started it up, and further assuming
Your day has been de *mierda*,
Place two hands on the wheel
Like the shoulders of that punk ass Bob in layout
You're finally going to give
A good goddamn shake to. Hunch up your back
And get all up in that invisible grill.
Mouth white-girl *muthafucka*
Like pre-dead Tupac to it as you get text-back
From your kid on his curfew, *Cunt* if you want
When the Versa before you brakes and a Big Mac
Slides through your fingers onto your Starters.
Find some pop on the radio: Pusha T is pissed enough
For ten of you so maybe you need to think backwards.
alt-J is good, The Bird and The Bee even better—
Why, oh, why do the bees need a beekeeper, that kind of shit
Meant to mellow your harsh
Will pop a cap in the ass of your amygdala.
Traffic? Crawl up that Mary Kay trunk and sit there
Until you can count the grey hairs
Of her junk backwards then fix her
With a death glare when you finally pass
Her that rips the pink from her Caddy.
Flick the bird at the guy at the stoplight
Flicking snot from his finger.
Caution is your go-to, right? But he's fucked you
Over with some skinny bitch from Supreme,
Called you out on your bullshit
In front of your bros.
So put the Vietnam Vet in your rearview
Along with his Dixie and teach him a *real* history lesson.
Vin Diesel it over the speed bumps.

Crow-fly to your ex's as if mad sex is
A huge magnet that pulls you through STOP signs and
Three lanes of assholes sipping lattes.
Pretend your Versa is a Humvee and the Jag with black
Windows a credible target as you introduce Lance Armstrong
There to Pavement, and while you're at it
Slice the homeless hag on the corner
A big piece of shame cake.
Blow through the light, the lot full of tots, the wreck
Of your life that is the emergency lane wide open
And fluorescent to the off ramp, a freeway
With no toll booths, the thin back
Of a Lyssa crusted with nails
Like the hide of a monster just like you.

Strip Mall, Locust Fork, Alabama:
Sign Above a Discount Mattress Store

"The Rest of Your Life"—
And the sudden thought as we roll through the STOP sign
Starred with bullet holes,
Necessita c'induce, e non diletto.

Yes, agrees the dog gnawing its tail outside,
The lone clerk wearing some sort of paper crown.
Too late. Too late.
You have lived your life the wrong way round.

Between Heaven and Hell

Granted, jet lag and three glasses of Sancerre
For breakfast, but still.

Between Heaven and Hell
Lies Paris? And that tone—

Auchinclossian, or de Beauvoir
Channeling Thurston Howell III.

Though something about the Limoges gravy boats
Scuttled in an armoire in ratty little *Le Jemmapes*

Seemed to agree to it, and it stuck with me
As we wobbled our way

Past bad rappers and Roma beggars on the sidewalk
With one leg tied back under their filthy skirts

Outside Chanel
To the Louvre, where *un vioc* with the faint lisp

Of the Languedoc roared *Terrorriste!*
At a woman in *hajib*

Staring in wonder at David's
The Lictors Bring to Brutus

the Bodies of His Sons.
Even the sky was yellow-gray

In a windy downpour
Before it turned sunny

In the Luxembourg Gardens
And kids' upturned smiling faces

Appeared like cancelled stamps
In the shadows of twigs

Along the path.
Not to mention the cemeteries

You insisted on spendy-taxiing to
Because each was "uniquely exquisite

And monstrous"
(Which you also said of the cottages

In Newport, by the way).
Monmartre, Montparanesse, Pere Lachaise

An hour before closing
Empty and about as inspiring as an Anglican church

On Tuesday. A slow march
Up one sodden *allée* and down the next

Until we found ourselves first like old giants—
Two fat gray-bearded Americans—

Lamenting the slim thighs of that bastard
Géricault. Then miniaturized, rolling Rave Kids reflected

Luminescent as glow sticks in the algaed water collected
In the serifs of pocked letters on the plinth.

Petrichor, but beneath it something acrid
Caught in the backs of our throats.

Needles, kind tins of cat food, an empty wallet
Emblazoned with pierced hearts. Until by God

Even the Devil himself—a *Sonderkommando*
In his black boots and striped jacket, humming

"Notre Espoir" *à la* Chevalier.
Heaps of the day's daffodils passing us

On his grounds man's cart,
Whispering on the way to the fire.

The Old Masters

Sometime late late last night, after polishing off
Two bottles of Millésime 2004
To mark our 25th wedding anniversary
And consequently finding ourselves dazed in bed
Face to face, eyelids drooping
With both reading lamps blazing,
Almost but not quite unconscious,
I wanted to exclaim as I once did
Something seriously corny,
Like *You are my queen!* or at least
Flatteringly stun you by reprising almost verbatim
Our first giddy grad school *interrogation*
Of Foucault's position on causal priority
Vis-à-vis madness
Over Rusty Nails at Café Dog,
Maybe dial up the time I was sick
And you sent me hand-pressed paper letters
Quoting Issa in the hospital.
But it wasn't happening.
And I got the sense
You wanted to do the same, salute my flagging cock
With an inspiring new pet name like *Le Chevalier*
Or insist as you strategically maneuvered your fingertips
Across my expanding forehead
I still looked like Bowie in his pre-Ziggy days.
But that wasn't happening either. Instead
What came out as far as I can remember
Was mostly just exhausted nonsense—
Bucket something something,
Vestibule something something,
As if each word weighed twenty pounds,
Hard to get a grip on.
Like heaving watermelons to a cute stranger
Over the side of a truck,

As we once did, broke and grunting
One morning outside Davenport, Iowa.
Or, no, like playing chess—O love has it come to this?—
On one of those giant chess sets at the mall.

Vine

I must have watched it twenty times
Before they took it down.
The one in the park on a bench
Where the kid in a blue hoodie
Shoots himself in the chest with a gun
He's showing off to his unseen friend
Who is giggling then gasps and a shriek
Starts up in her throat but stops.
The tock! and the little hole flapping open
In his shirt where the blood will leak out
In tendrils that climb down
The twin posts of his pants—
But not yet. Not yet.

I must have watched it twenty times, studying
The shadows, the shape of a cloud, trying to
Imagine my way into those six seconds thrown
Up on the Internet that morning
Before finally giving up and returning to my book.
One of the Penguins from the seventies
With a short piece from a dour Swedish poet
That had the word *abeyance* in it and black trees;
At the end, a long prison wall receding
Into the vanishing point, and if I'm not mistaken
The strangled cry of a bird
A passerby hears and moves on.

Toro

Everything moves toward silence, toward emptiness,
Says the great Jersey poet mid-mai tai's
On the open terrace
Of the old Tampa Bay Hotel—
He's a bull at 83 but disappearing
Before my eyes, rheumy, arthritic, fighting a head cold.
Keats, Machado, Cage, Picard, Merton—
You know how you have to sit there
As your father who once seemed so magical, so strong,
Reels off the lineup of the '43 Dodgers
For the 100th time? There was some of that.
But also this: his hands
Suddenly jutting into the puddle of candlelight,
One flattened knuckle
Describing a palette knife
Scraping the back of a canvas
To illustrate the muddled fur
And fine hairs Picasso sketched in
The first draft of one of his *toros*—
these details which the artist
*Would inevitably remove, until…*and then
Let's call him Robert rearing back
To slash five surprisingly savage
Strokes between us that were its flanks, its back,
Forelegs and lowered head, as if wordless
With one raised finger
Emerging from his handkerchief he'd speared
A constellation down from the humid stars
To stand before us,
That snorted once and disappeared.

Natural Selection

In the frozen food section,
Each section lights up as I pass.
Blueberry mini-muffins, stout pierogis, little
Pouches of mauve fondant—
Like hearing one birdcall at a time.
All the vanished species
Of the earth rising up out of the ice
Again to sing into the clear untouchable air.
Darkness ahead, darkness behind.

Books and Correspondences: Leviathan, Thomas Hobbes

"… and the life of man, solitary, poor, nasty, brutish, and short."

My nephew loves the cover—that leering Burger
King, inked up—or Bam Margera wearing bees?

Rubs it like a magic lamp.
Mumblerapped for weeks the famous phrase

Like a spell cast over every goddamn thing
From bowls of lime Jello to birthday vintage Vans

(Asperger's, his parents announced, like sommeliers,
With a breath of ADD)

Until last night it found me, too, in a dream,
Each word transformed

Into a ghostly name-like name
On a blown up county map I put a ghostly finger on:

Tough-luck coal towns deep in West Virginia
Where I'd spent hours on dreary summer Sundays

Shack by shack
Politely sipping brackish Hyssop tea

In scorching kitchens like a little prince
Sent out to cheer the locals,

Admiring a quaint parade of whittled
Horse-shaped things

And marveling at the cornball strangeness in my lap:
All those distant doomed dumbass kin

Called "Lamentation," "Helpless," or, really, "Ashes"—
Rowed down yellowed Bible fronts

By cartoon brides I dolled in feedbag frocks
And squirrel-eyed Pa's who fucked their pigs.

How long ago was that?
Thirty years? Thirty-five?

I think my family crest will be a prick
Erect beneath the motto *semper crudelis semper stultus.*

"*Contempt,*" wrote Hobbes, in Paris, in pen and ink
He carried in a cudgel-cane's hollowed head,

*"Or little sense of the calamity of others, is that which men
Call CRUELTY; proceeding from Security of their own fortune."*

E.g., the book Josh raps me on the knee
With suddenly this morning, would have me, too,

Rub like a magic lamp. Recoil. Wipe chin.
"You've spilled my coffee."

E.g, in sophomore year, in California, tan and
Fat on dead Dad's money

How I hollowed out the thing unread
And hid my stash there.

Down in the Mangroves

There's a pelican standing on one leg
Like a burnt-out light bulb.
And the low voice of a man like a far-off train
Reflected in ditch water.
The sounds of cars on the highway—
A bear with its head caught in a bucket.
There's a suitcase with a little girl's body inside.
The feeling of having forgotten
Something at the store
Is mostly what the soul is, right?
The bare patch rubbed raw on a cat's paw—
For some, that's the soul, too.
Maybe the killer's.
His hands are like two famous brothers
Who hate each other.
His days flap open like the coat of someone running,
Days like lost dogs.
There's a pink condom and a hairweave
Like symbols in a Renaissance painting,
And one of those red rubber coin purses
Like the mouth on Señor Wences' hand.
When a breeze fills up a plastic bag
It's like the stupefied face of a puppet in a jack-in-the box.
There's the smell of meat-smoke from a barbecue
Like a lampshade with a red nightgown thrown over it.
Also a bleached green button
And a sunglass lens perfectly round
Side by side like a double sun rising above an airless planet
On the cover of a nostalgic science fiction novel.
In the distance there's the squawking of seagulls
Bitter to the ear like the taste of aspirin.
There's a manatee out there, too, like a prehistoric baby.
There's the sky like the pleathered flesh of a dolphin.
And the invisible presence of the stars
Together with their constellations

That form sea monsters, peacocks, and carpenter's levels,
Along with the yet to be discovered outlines
Of iPhones and the visages of pop stars and butchers.
When the waves retreat there is the trembling
Of thousands of seashells
Like the silence in a hallway
Where someone's just finished hollering,
There's a can of peaches that looks right at you.
Its top is open, there's a knife
With a plastic handle sticking out,
White like the smell of Christmas
Ornaments kept in a box.
If you think she's like the last peach,
Deliquescing in its juices,
That's on you.

Metope, Tagalog, Raskolnikov

And to all the other read but never or too late heard
Words and names I've mispronounced
Over the years
I apologize most sincerely

And for your prompt and scholarly corrections
Offered so generously strictly in the interests of accuracy
Without regard for circumstance or company
As language demands of course
O my tireless erstwhile tutors—
Beginning with hip Sister Margaret
Who played "Phil Oaks" for us
And especially you dear colleague M,
Fond of referring with the utmost assurance
To Hilliard's seminal *minitures*—
I ask humbly of whoever is in charge of such matters
That when you die you return to this earth circa 1012
In the person of Tang Su
Who while dining at the court of the Emperor
Laid down his chopsticks pointing east rather than west
And so was dragged by his hair from the chambers
Into seventeen years of penal solitude
In the freezing dust-choked provinces
Where he gobbled pig-slop with his fingers
And even the chickens
Turned in disgust their thin faces from him.

Race Relations

The young mothers are beside themselves with grief,
The shirt-sleeved young reporter is saying; also
"Joy ride" and "believed to be." Nice hair,
Bright teeth, but in the spots at the scene fresh acne flares
Big as jujubes stuck on his chin. Behind him

Aside from the gathered tats and flipflops
The usual suspects: idling wrecker, buff cops, a crumpled
Corolla fished from the drink. More black
Kids pedaling around on their high-bars as gaffed
Key Latch palms stalk off in place in the breezy night.

Then a long shot of the real monster, the dark
Retention pond, which as any Floridian will tell you
Aren't ponds at all but huge sewers
Dredged in the '40s to take on the overflow from our wild,
House-lashing storms; planted everywhere

With Golden Canna, Spikerush, any deep rooted thing
To hold back the constant erosion, absorb our shit, lead,
Chlordane and cadmium, while leaving the cute otters
And gold carp in peace at least until the big one finally blows.

Walk Out of Yourselves!

Jerry half-shouts, Walk out of yourselves
At the end of each session.
Big bald Fester-head, arms extended, wriggling
White fingers—ooga-booga!
Walk out of yourself!
As if everyone didn't, every day,
Pulling on their Dockers and new Spanx,
Mostrando un poco de teta al nuevo propietario.
As if we hadn't walked out of ourselves
Just to get *here*—stepping over dead babies,
Crack dads, young girls with one leg in Fallujah,
Just to get *here*—a crumbling basement
Supply Room cleaned out in the old Y
Set every Monday with yes folding chairs and a table
Of stale cookies and weak coffee.
Wanting what everyone wants, Jerry—
To walk back into themselves,
Lock the door,
Lie back on the couch in their own house in the dark
For a few minutes, alone in one body.

Segway

Morning, and these stiff charioteers,
Repeated in profile,
On the boardwalk in Clearwater, Florida—
Burger stands, shivering *chicas*, pit bulls.
A trap door opens inside me.
The Gulf of Mexico is the desert.
The tourists are the Pharaohs.
This is the afterlife.

A Facebook Diorama

Consisting entirely of a rough watercolor
      cardboard box loggia
With sketched-in tiles and columns where

A bored blue-robed calico curls up beneath
A Christmas tree's white angel, poised
      on fishing line just above her head:

Gabriel, of course, translucent, flared-winged,
      announcing you-know-what
To his red-eyed feline Mary.

      The shadow of the Maker's hand.

Querying the Hive Mind

(adapted from posts on MetaFilter)

Trees in fields. Why? Why
Are there solitary trees in the middle of fields?
The writer asks. He's desperate. (Why?)
The board's abuzz with answers.
Shade for livestock. Shade for farmers. A roost
For flying pest control. Hawks and owls.
A landmark or a marker. A thing to piss on.
It's picturesque—a paid-for photo op, perhaps?.
To mark a water-source? Lumber? Fruit?
Have you ever tried
To uproot a tree? It's not easy work.
You gotta cut the bulk of it down
And chop up the trunk and branches.
Then you have to dig around the stump
Deep enough to get a chain around it
And find a piece of equipment
Muscular enough to pull the stump out.
(If you have no dynamite.) Write it down:
When the thunderstorm rolls in on you, you'll be glad
You aren't the highest object in the field.
A low wet spot that can't be farmed, an old well,
A cattle pen. Whatever. Random. Say

An animal ate something in one place
And shat out the seeds.
What would happen?
Gravestones are the culprit, I suspect.
People plant a tree right beside them.
Fifty years later, the tree is huge
And the roots heave the headstone into gravel.
But ask the farmer.
It could be the place he first made love.
(Or killed the UPS guy.)

Rural folks and farmers are sentimental.
Decisions are not always practical.
Here in Ireland, we have a fear of "Fairy Trees."
Also, Iceland.
Someone applied a Fourier transform to a forest,
And wound up with a Dirac delta function tree.
Thank you! Thank you! Writes the writer.
Great answers! Thank you! Except
I do not understand the last one.

4

Transmission

—to Gellu Naum

... black bloody claws stuck shoulder–high:
violence, anguish, absence.
And one must consider also the tree. Imagine
There is an underground mycorrhizal
Network weaving hyphae
Finer than old men's hair root-to-root
At a cellular level (there is),
A wood-wide web where druggy maples trade tips
On where to scrounge the best free sugars,
Stately sycamores kibitz, cavil
About the sorry state of bulk pore space,
Fret about aphids (they do).
Though it's not all scary, or quotidian.
A dying birch offers everything it was
So a seedling might get a little sunshine;
The neighbors chip in, too.
How far can we be
From the human sensation of grief, or joy?
Now about those claw marks:
A wound to the one who left them
As to their receptor. The awful news
Announced with a howl.
A soughing of limbs, that sudden
Furious murmur of leaves in windless fields.

A Poetry Reading on the Patio Outside the Tallahassee Room of the St. Petersburg Public Library

—for Robert Bly

Out of fashion now, but even then
Only a dozen of us or so, drowsy
In our summer finery of shorts and flipflops,
Sieving sweat through
Our pocket tees as we drove with you shotgun
Ensorcelled by the swirling snow
On deserted Main Street to post a letter;
To clasp the iron handle
Of the mailbox and think about the word *privacy.*

1968. All the world was war and stunned roses
Ferried across fuscous hallways
To the televised wounded but
Inside us, in those minutes, God,
How your gold animals
Were a miracle, roaming
The dry pastures of the eternal
Full of joy, their gentle movements
A kind of bare medieval music
That leapt down the magnolia leaves
and lit up our skulls.
O, many exclamation marks!
O, hesitations of unseen dashes—
O, questions leaping up in us like cold flames.
Where might the soul's flock of sparrows
Light for the night, Master?
Which direction the dark tires' track,
Where what castle of grief, how the hair's asylum?
So many clouds, so many lonely harbors,
Buckets, hammocks
And cornfields, crickets invisible

Under box-elder leaves to praise!
So much wind and rain—a storm
Of marvelous images blowing sideways
From your mouth we disappeared into:
Moles with golden wings,
Snowflakes like *the jewels of a murdered Gothic prince.*
And for a moment you, too, Robert,
Vanished, eyes closed before us
In private reverie, a hypnotist
Fallen under his own spell. The one you cast
And woke at last from, dazed
But utterly happy in Misssoula, Montana, whispering
Thank you, thank you.

Endless Tuesday

In the break room
No one wants to hear
The brainless avid one trill it—
The -ex, the new Trex, the weak latte,
The mind-blowing glaciers,
The broken child or the break-in.
It's like we're all ten, bored, left alone,
Waiting for nothing
But our grandmother's cuckoo clock
In the sweltering den to reveal the hour again—
The one someone wound too tight at the factory.
And here it comes.
The news of its news arriving on that dumb face
Before he opens his mouth.

Remedy

Up late one night a few years ago
I was scared, balled up, thinking about death.
So what else? I Googled it but after cessation
Of biological functions, fifty GIFS and a TED talk
On the curious way repeated playings of *Xenoblade*
Help survivors cope with grief,
I was looking for something a little meatier
And typed in Death Poetry.
Merwin: *The dead go away like bruises.*
I am the yellow finch that came to her feeder, chirped Mary Ruefle.
Et cetera. Fine, but it was like
Attending a very nice funeral for death.
Or a wake. It was like the fall night in grad school
We all got high and jammed
Into the famous melancholy poet's writing shed
Where one by one his breathy Languedoc widow
Had us recite something *ravissant* by her husband;
For a few moments a kind of adrenalized dread
Filled that space as we coughed up
Our words and watched them
Shamble off into the pines through the window.
And that was pretty much that.
Until I remembered how when it was his turn
The great man's superwrecked
Old Serbian pal Z had reared back and hurled
Four mostly incomprehensible lines
Like an ancient blood oath to the bare rafters.
"И није смрт оно што боли…" God,
The sight of him—tall as a bear,
Roseate, mustachioed, rocking
A Greek sailor's cap and a pair of Earth shoes;
He could have stepped out of a Bulajić movie.
Later we heard him and Marguerite tearing tickets
Under the picnic table in the side garden.

As I say, a few years ago, anxious, up late.
Though ever since, I have to admit,
I've felt a little better about things.

To Some Non-Letters, Praise

For italics tonight in a book by Chistyakov
That make *the iron birches* tipsy and **bold letters**
With !!!!!! and glitter on my niece's pink-paper
Note to Kwae her new BFF
Not to mention the dash—useful for example
In describing how it flut-ter-ed as it fell
To the kitchen floor from her Hello Kitty backpack
Praise for the atmark @ a pitcher's wind-up a galaxy
A blood-knot in one eye a partly pared apple
Praise the asterisk * a caution I should have printed up
On little cards to hand out like deaf-mutes
Used to back in the day whenever I promise anything to anyone
Praise for the hashtag # along with $'s and /'s
Standing in for shit and goddamn in ancient comic books
And praise for the caret ^ a mountain peak without a mountain
As for the arms akimbo < > without a body
Praise for the = that is never and the % that is always
Praise too for the lowly comma,
The size of an eyelash or a week-old fetus
Though the Oxford variety of which omitted
From a contract's obscure clause
Regarding overtime cost thieving Oakhurst Dairy millions
All praise for the rare tilde ~ a horseman's trailing cape
Or perhaps the shivering underwater wake of a dolphin
But most of all praise now as I press SHIFT to strike
The beautiful question mark ?
And see before me the naked female form
Whether standing or recumbent
Or is it a proboscis above a doodled cleft chin
A raised jai alai *xistera* in any case
The true if unacknowledged end punctuation
Of all sentences, let's face it

King of Pain

Imagine: a motel tryst. Winter Break, Key West,
Eighties. She the student, he the sturdy blond but balding
Almost yet quite clearly not quite hip adjunct French Lit
Professor/poet stiff shot of Bacardi to her mollies,
Who almost cries when she shrugs, Yeah.

The rum—of course. The rum, the ghastly room,
The freeze-dried art, her bra defused in a stew of slurred
Reproches doux followed by more rum and that hum again.
Thong a mess of cherry spit-up on his chest, the sting
Of stubble on her neck like turpentine, the Brut, the furtive
Finger up her bum. And now for some
Of that Tantric sex he's read about in *Interview*—

But, no. Screwing her six slow ways to Nirvana
Is fun but fun denied, and no Viagra yet.
Still, sans alibi. No Department wreck or starter *crise*, no
Pop-up wife. Just that unplaced hum of his she hears
Whispered now back again
As he stands before the open first-floor window,
The empty bottle tipped from his lips then spun
Clockwise on the desk as on a rec-room floor
Where eager faces flare. One outstretched finger
Pointing to the burned-out star atop the giant Christmas
Palm in the cobbled square, the star that is he sings
She'll swear his *soul up there.*

Poem with Horse and RB

This is the poem where no one drowns in summer
Or propranolol, gyves or sluices
Or falls in love with Sister Wendy.
No one pisses off a dock, no one is pixilated
No one wakes this morning
Believing her life is like
The reassembled pieces of a torn-up letter,
Nothing clots or tethers.
This is the poem where no one fingers
A violet scar on the back of a cowboy's neck,
No one pleasures
Herself in the rank nest of her father's deer stand.
Nothing is pale, nothing shattered or bedizened.
This is the poem that does not collage, appropriate,
Ventriloquize Frank O'Hara or holla, that does not try
To squeeze into the skinny jeans of erasures or pantoums.
This is the poem from which
The ornate nomenclature of ornithology,
Minerology, cytomorphology and all the other ologies
Is absent, together with the word "absent";
In which nothing scuds.
There are no tufts, and sex is not *like* anything
Except perhaps a brief shriek down a forever
Recycling water slide.
This is the poem that does not keen the passing
Of passenger trains
Or Mr. Furman my fifth-grade teacher.
This is the poem without scent, without footsteps.
In other words this is the poem that closes the door
And locks itself in behind it.
No castanets, no pie, no Dachau or *luminescent*,
No hickies or Sweet Jesus, no animals whatsoever.
Well, maybe one. Because how strange,
How cynical and impoverished
Would a poem have to be to refuse admittance to a horse?

And while we're at it, while he's still around, say,
Good old Robert Bly to see it with such clear eyes,
The white flake of snow that has just fallen on its mane.

The Poetry Assessor

Into which you enter your poem,
Click "calculate," and sit back while an algorithm
Of computational linguistics
Decides its fate: "professional" or "amateur"
Broadly speaking,
As denoted by something called a Logit score.
For example, "Working Late"—Louis Simpson's
Hard work earns top honors at 0.93,
While Galway Kinnell, out squeezing and squinching
For his breakfast, dawdles in at 0.06
With "Blackberry Eating"—dead last
But happy, one assumes. James Dickey's "Adultery"?
A mediocre 0.54. (Smack dab between "Scar"
By Lucille Clifton and James Wright's "A Blessing.")

Sad? Okay, sad. But what was sadder still
Was that I found out
About all this—where else?—on Facebook,
In a not quite well-known poet's post
To a Friend that humblebragged
She had "succumbed and pasted the first poem
of my new book into the Poetry Assessor. It scored .89,
just two steps down from Plath's 'Crossing the Water.'
I can live with that." Smiley face.

See?

Still, an ego-stroke. To be pitched skyward
As on some poetry trampoline
Above Sharon Olds, Ai, and Frank O'Hara!
Donald Justice? Gary Snyder? Sure, if you say so!
You're the Poetry Assessor, after all, one can almost hear
Her squeak. But then again, can she really?
Live with it, I mean. Isn't it also easy to imagine
Her wide awake at 4 a.m., peering up into that still

Starry-er firmament and silently contemplating the rank
Injustice of falling short of the likes of Billy
Collins, say, and of the taste of ashes
That would linger on her tongue?
"Japan"? Really? She could've written that one
In the time it took to eat those goddamn grapes.

Over Northern Virginia
October 18, 2016

—*from* Emails to a Young Poet

This one's for Frank, my bar-mate at Appleby's,
As at 35,000 feet I still see and overhear myself shouting "Say
Hello to Delores!" toward a receding Stetson in the full flush
Of four Dos Equis and "Promise!" as we head
For our separate gates after our little Bro Tango of Trump
And Big Twelve football that somehow clacked
Its four Merrells right off the dance floor
Into the starry dynamo of the machinery of night.

Or was it Dora? Anyway, although somehow
I don't envision you as the type to be caught cowering
In unshaven rooms in your underwear,
Or burning cigarette holes in your arms protesting
The narcotic tobacco-haze of Capitalism,
I could be wrong.
A great poet if not an angleheaded hipster
Might be slouching under that luxe salesman get-up.

Okay. Maybe not a *great* poet.
Though not terrible, either. Like most of us
You have your moments.
I'm thinking of the best one, about the otters.
Their steady gaze upon me like the blank pages of old calendars.
I'm not sure what it means, but I sense something wise here,
Something *zazen* that doesn't do time or regret.
Or maybe I'm jealous.
The otters I've met have mostly taken one look at me
And skedaddled. The little pouches under their arms
Where they keep spare rocks to hammer
Open sea urchin shells, you say,
I didn't know that. It reminds me

Suddenly of my great-uncle Alejandro, whom I adored,
A hairy little man with big enemies who carried a derringer
In his pocket through the dim alleys of Cicero, Illinois.
And who would have thought *romp* or *raft*
Was their group name, that some, contra the sea urchins,
Are actually ovo-vegetarians?
Do you know the word *sapiosexual?*
It means a person who finds intelligence
To be the most attractive
Feature in a human being. Noble, but in the end doomed.
The first girl I kissed on the lips
Was a budding fifteen-year-old Egyptologist.
Her thin tongue slithered in my mouth like a dry hieroglyph
For a few seconds, and that was that.
Enter her cousin, lithe big-breasted Ophilia.
What I mean is, these otterfacts are good things to know,
But not the lingering scent of Jean Naté
On your neck, not one ragged unpainted toenail.
They lack privacy, and magic.

What else? The word "empire." Not to nitpick, but while
I can imagine myself as an otter
On the shore bowing to an OtterKing waving his paw
When he floated by on his back, I'm not sure
How his *fur regalia* would be different from mine.
Would he sport epaulettes and a crown of some kind,
Like a cartoon or do you mean in the Orwellian sense
All otters are kings
But some are kingly-er than others, smarter or fatter,
Their coats glossier, perhaps? (Explore!)
And wouldn't he be on top of, not inside, the *royal carriage*
Of the river?
Then things really go haywire.
In stanza three, *the black fluidity of space /*
In the amphorae of their frontal lobes

Sounds to me like Heraclitus
And Arthur C. Clarke have been standing a little too close
In the poetry elevator. And how does this relate
To consciousness, exactly? By the time a few lines
Later we get to the giant—your father—and his shirt front
Confetti'd with scattered Pall Mall flakes,
You've lost me. The otter has left the building.

So, Frank. (Imagine me putting on my editor's hat.)
Unfortunately, like the other ones— "Erect Sky" "Sioux, Me" —
"Loneliness with Otters," is not for us.
(And now taking it off again.)
Maybe it's not for anybody.
What I mean is—how to say it? I'm no horticulturist
But a few days ago I was leafing through
One of my wife's International Field Guides

And came across an orchid called *Rhizanthella gardneri*—
Dime-sized, apparently it lives its entire life unseen,
Compressed in underground crevices in Western Australia
Where over generations its scent develops wild, unheard of
Intensities many multiples of the common rose.
Does that help? Or what's the line—
The bird the painter doesn't paint
That makes the whole sky bluer. Something like that.
(On a personal note, decades ago, I did a good thing,
A small thing, involving black ice and a station wagon
Full of teenagers, but told no one: just the thought of it
All these years has been like a nightlight in the back of my
brain, illuminating some pretty dark stairs,
A lot of gray, solemn afternoons.)

Anyway, sorry—gotta run, Buddy.
I can see the lights of EWR
From my window seat—Christmas ornaments

Smashed to smithereens.
Gotta unplug, gather up all these goddamn cords,
Stuff them into my
Computer case and text my brother-in-law.
By now, I'd guess you're halfway to that convention in Omaha.
Maybe you're thinking about Delores
Or Dora, scarfing peanuts, maybe starting to write
Another poem inspired by the curlicued
Blue ribbon on the woman's head
Crowning over the seat in front of you, the way it bobs
Like an amberjack lure in the steady stream
Of cold air rushing from the little nozzle—I can see that.
But, Frank: don't. Leave that woman's head alone.
Just this once, for me, permit that ribbon
To unfurl unmolested with all the majesty
It can muster, which is a lot.
Remember what I said about the flower,
The bird, and the good thing—the power
Of compound interest is astonishing in the inner life, too.
What did Oscar Wilde say? *Only secrecy*
Makes modern life mysterious or marvelous.

       Yours,
       Daniel

Reading Rilke

The long slow bow of want
To must, this life, my dashing poet-Da
Would spout, trailing off into rheumy et cetera
Et ceteras, footsteps heavy on the sighing
Staircase. He drank, of course, hit us, my Ma,
The cat when he could catch her,
Wore splotched patches
On his coat sleeves as his hangdog profs had
His first and last year at frowsy Clongowes Wood;
Puffed cadged Hambone from a straight flush
Meerschaum half-bent
As he declaimed his way around the Village
Bars where by his dim lights he was a Local Legend
Well-known to swoon
Even those *stupid German bitches* from their britches
In the loo with his dour doomed Irish bard
Shtick (and their fat-arsed husbands stood him
Rounds of Rheingold).

63—by the clock tonight I see I am officially his age
When he died, glazed, half-mad, heaving
Blood and bile down
The front steps of St. Mary's. Tonight, yes—
1,432 days clean and still finding fresh traces
Of his face in mine in the bathroom mirror,
Shivering as I return to that *poof* Rilke—
outflowing, river-like, with deltas
that spread like arms to reach the open sea …
Listen my heart, as only saints
have listened …
The upstairs study quiet, all asleep,
Outside the velvet lawn bowed beneath the wanting
Stars: you must not change your life.

A Clue, A Sign, A Bad Omen

Is what she thinks in sequence,
As in the tot-park she spots
An ivory lady's leather driving glove
Pointing one finger at the rain-glazed see-saw.
Inside, her boy whose neck might, falling, snap there,
Sees nothing much, only octaves
Of light and grey. His mother's voice a riddle,
Endlessly repeating. But for how long
Will I have him?
Ten years, one, a day? she worries
As she stirs pink shrimp into broken ramen.
Not hungry. Still. Spoon and slurp.
Eating is the best thing. The jingle-jangle of the radio,
Early Dylan, *evening's empire has returned into sand.*
Maybe later a few pages of She, the white queen Ayesha
With her veils and telegnosis—for once to be desired
Like that, obeyed by any damn thing. Now she's trying
To remember what the doctor said, *vitamins, keep yourself calm,*
Relax. That's the most important thing.
Nothing's happened yet—her prayer-flag flapping inside her.
My feet hurt, my back. Pink urine. Yellow bruise on my breast?
Am I crazy? Fright emoji. No answer yet. Resend.
In the meantime she surveys the kitchen.
Cute swishing black cat clock's tail.
Porcelain salt shaker, Lil's or Harry's? Beautiful
Etched robin statuette, some color-word
Must attach to you, but which? Pewter? Tin?
You with the ring and the house key
Secreted in your belly when I lift
Off your top half, tell me.
Does your missing one yellow eye
Portend something awful?
Will my baby boy die of it?
I think you know. The answer please:
I have lots of keys but open no doors. *What is this?*

Midpoint

At the midpoint
Of my life I didn't feel I was in a submarine
Silently crossing the International Date Line,
Nor get the sense of cinder-stitched *allées* stretching out
Between shadowy walls of phosphorescent foliage.
And I definitely didn't see myself as a granite statue
Beating itself into an idea with a granite hammer.
Maybe I heard birdsong, but no bird.
Or maybe I was the bird and my birdsong
Was this: cries from some childhood playground,
A dull dental-work ache like a provincial orchestra
Tuning up in my veins. Chair scrapes
Followed by the roar of a gem-polishing machine.
The number 42, 42, 42, pronounced in Esperanto
As if a freezing prisoner in a courtyard
Was pleading for his life—
Kvardek du, kvardek du, kvardek du.
And, of course, the headwinds, howling in
From the North, starting to make a weathervane creak
Beneath a galloping horse that stands perfectly still.

Acknowledgments

Grateful acknowledgment is made to the editors of the following journals, in which a number of these poems originally appeared, a few in slightly revised versions:

American Journal of Poetry: "Central State Hospital Visit, October, 1962," "The Memory of My Memory is My Memory," "Driving Lessons: How to Drive (Angry)," "The Old Woman Hit by a Truck," "Between Heaven and Hell," "Dear Dewi," "Poem with Horse and RB," "Endless Tuesday," and "Young Squirrel"

Adirondack Review: "Wig Shop Choir"

The Asheville Review: "Books and Correspondences: Leviathan, Thomas Hobbes" and "Phantom Limb"

B O D Y: "Metope, Tagalog, Raskolnikov," "Down in the Mangroves" and "Segway"

The Common: "Exusciatatio," "Books and Correspondences: A Short History of Decay, E.M. Cioran," "Natural Selection" and "Velda the Seer"

Chamber 4: "Unknown Destination"

Cortland Review: "The Gun My Sister Killed Herself With," "A Facebook Diorama" and "At a Dig In Kent"

decomP: "Depression" and " Midpoint"

diode: "Transmission" and "Untitled, But Maybe"

FIELD: "Vine"

Live Encounters: "Natural Selection," "Sign Above a Discount Mattress Store," "Flense" and "Shquiver"

Manhattan Review: "To the Motherland" and "View from a Treehouse"

The Meadow: "Querying the Hive Mind"

Marsh Hawk Review: "Schizophrenia" and "Ant"

Modern Haiku: "buzz of the streetlamp ..."

Numero Cinq: "Up Late" and "Portrait of My Father"

Prairie Schooner: "A" and "Antoinette in Flames'

PiF Magazine: "In the Alzheimer's Ward at Saint Jude's"

Ploughshares: "The Old Masters" and "The Dean Has No Comment"

Prick of the Spindle: "Gazebo"

Solstice: "*Dépaysement* " "1982"

SN Review: "The Shoes of the Old Ones" and "Squat"

SurVision: "Walk Out of Yourself"

Many thanks to so many who helped make this book possible—
Siobhán Hutson and Jessie Lendennie of Salmon Poetry Press; editor
Marc Vincenz of MadHat Press; David Breskin, whose guidance and
encouragement were invaluable; publicist Mary Bisbee-Beek; Isabel
Breskin for layout and editing support; Tyler Finck of The League of
Moveable Type, for his display font, League Mono; and to Chelsea Hadley
of The Shifting Foundation.

DANIEL LAWLESS is the founder and editor of the monthly online magazine *Plume: A Journal of Contemporary Poetry*, and the *Plume* anthologies, which appear in print annually. His poems have been published in *Ploughshares*, *Prairie Schooner*, *FIELD*, and *The American Journal of Poetry*, among many others. Lawless has lived and taught in France and the UK, and now resides in St. Petersburg, Florida. He writes critical essays and conducts author interviews. He received a grant from The Shifting Foundation in 2018. *Louisville 1984-1974*, is the title of his forthcoming book, comprising a number of prose poems and sketches drawing on his youthful experiences in that city.

Author Photo by Donna Lawless

www.**salmon**poetry.com

"Like the sea-run Steelhead salmon that thrashes upstream to its spawning ground,
then instead of dying, returns to the sea – Salmon Poetry Press
brings precious cargo to both Ireland and America in the poetry it publishes,
then carries that select work to its readership against incalculable odds."

TESS GALLAGHER